PRECIOUS TIME
CHILDREN LIVING WITH MUSCULAR DYSTROPHY

DON'T
TURN
AWAY

For a free color catalog describing Gareth Stevens' list of high-quality books and multimedia programs, call 1-800-542-2595 (USA) or 1-800-461-9120 (Canada). Gareth Stevens Publishing's Fax: (414) 225-0377. See our catalog, too, on the World Wide Web: http://gsinc.com

Library of Congress Cataloging-in-Publication Data
Bergman, Thomas, 1947-
    [En kamp för framtiden. English]
    Precious time : children living with muscular dystrophy /
by Thomas Bergman. -- North American ed.
        p. cm. -- (Don't turn away)
    Includes index.
    Summary: Describes the life, including medical attention and various daily
activities, of a nine-year-old boy with Duchenne muscular dystrophy.
    ISBN 0-8368-1597-1 (lib. bdg.)
    1. Duchenne muscular dystrophy--Juvenile literature. [1. Duchenne muscular
dystrophy. 2. Diseases.] I. Title. II. Series: Bergman, Thomas, 1947-
Don't turn away.
RJ482.D78B4713 1996
362.1'9892748--dc20   96-5726

Don't Turn Away
Determined to Win: Children Living with Allergies and Asthma
Finding a Common Language: Children Living with Deafness
Going Places: Children Living with Cerebral Palsy
Meeting the Challenge: Children Living with Diabetes
Moments that Disappear: Children Living with Epilepsy
On Our Own Terms: Children Living with Physical Disabilities
One Day At A Time: Children Living with Leukemia
Precious Time: Children Living with Muscular Dystrophy
Seeing in Special Ways: Children Living with Blindness
We Laugh, We Love, We Cry: Children Living with Mental Retardation

D O N 'T
T U R N
A W A Y

First published in North America in 1996 by
Gareth Stevens Publishing
1555 North RiverCenter Drive, Suite 201
Milwaukee, WI 53212 USA

Published in Sweden under the title *En kamp för framtiden*.

© 1996 this format by Gareth Stevens, Inc.
Photographs and original text © 1996 by Thomas Bergman.
Additional text and design © 1996 by Gareth Stevens, Inc.

Editor: Barbara J. Behm
Series designer: Kate Kriege

Special thanks to Carol Sowell of the Muscular Dystrophy Association for her assistance with the accuracy of the text.

Printed in the United States of America

1 2 3 4 5 6 7 8 9 99 98 97 96

PRECIOUS TIME

CHILDREN LIVING WITH MUSCULAR DYSTROPHY

Thomas Bergman

Gareth Stevens Publishing
MILWAUKEE

*A*ll parents want their children to be healthy. But life does not always turn out as we wish. In this book, I tell the story of nine-year-old Stefan. I followed Stefan with my camera for a year — at home, at school, and at the hospital. From his birth, he has had a disease called Duchenne muscular dystrophy. The disease makes Stefan's muscles weaker and weaker as time goes by.

Stefan and all other children in the same situation have a right to be happy. We must give them all the support and opportunities they so greatly deserve.

Stefan is taking part in a research project that has made him more active and left him feeling a little better than usual. Whether the medicine will make his muscles stronger remains to be seen. Until then, we must not give up hope. Hope is the last thing the children give up, and we must do everything possible to give them a bright future.

I am very grateful to Stefan and his family for letting me reveal his life in photos and text. I also want to thank Dr. Mia Hovmöller at the children's clinic at Karolinska Hospital in Stockholm, Sweden, for helping me with the information, and Christina Mandley at the Muscle Dystrophy Foundation in Stockholm, Sweden, for all her advice.

Thomas Bergman

Thomas Bergman

*I*t is a very special occasion when we can present our readers with another title in the Don't Turn Away series. Precious Time *introduces you to Stefan, a courageous young man with muscular dystrophy.*

Thomas Bergman's deeply moving photography reveals a boy who valiantly lives his life each day to the fullest. You'll see Stefan canoeing, steering a truck, driving his wheelcar, playing with his dog, and throwing a Frisbee. Stefan's physical limitations cannot stop his spirit. He is an inspiration to us all.

Gareth Stevens

Gareth Stevens
Publisher

STEFAN

Stefan is a nine-year-old boy who makes his home in Stockholm, Sweden. He lives with his parents and his little sister, Sandra. Stefan has a muscle disease. Until Stefan was two years old, he was so weak that his mother always had to carry him in her arms. He started to walk at just over two, but his walk was unsteady. He often stumbled. Stefan's doctor examined him very carefully and took blood and muscle samples. Tests confirmed that Stefan has a congenital muscle disease called muscular dystrophy — the Duchenne type. The doctor told Stefan's parents that the disease would make Stefan's muscles weaker and weaker, eventually disabling him. Stefan's parents were very sad.

Stefan has a dream. When he grows up, he wants to be a truck driver just like his father. The family operates a small trucking firm with three trucks.

Stefan often plays with his trucks while waiting for his dad to come home. This afternoon, Stefan goes with his father on a delivery. His father lifts Stefan up into the driver's cab and fastens the seat belt. After they make the delivery, Stefan sits in his father's lap.

"Dad, can I steer the truck?" Stefan asks. Because they are driving safely on a back road, Stefan's dad agrees to it. Stefan sings with joy as he steers, looking proudly out of the cab.

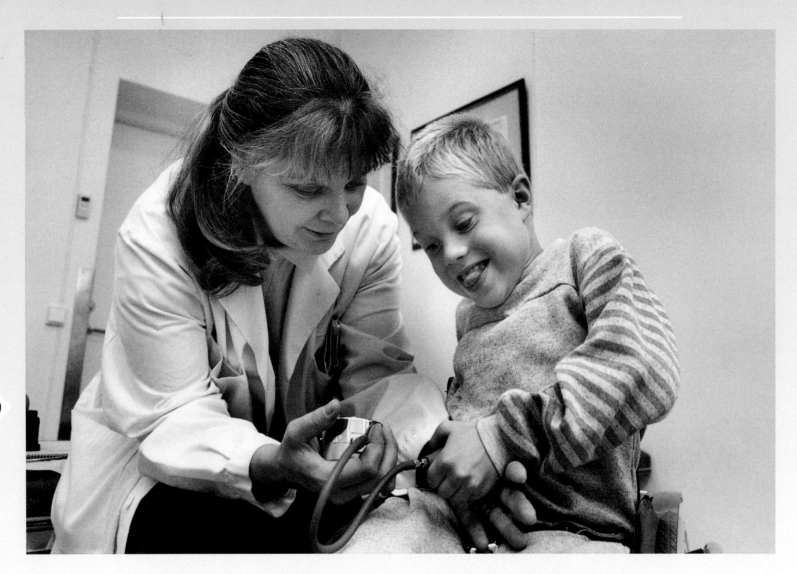

Every fourth month, Stefan goes to the hospital to see Dr. Mia Hovmöller. Each visit, Dr. Mia measures and weighs Stefan and examines him carefully. Dr. Mia asks Stefan and his mother if there have been any changes since the last visit. Stefan's mother says that Stefan's arms and legs are getting weaker and that he often falls.

Dr. Mia examines Stefan's ability to move his hands, arms, shoulders, legs, and ankles. She also looks at his Achilles tendons. Then, she measures the strength of the muscles in Stefan's hands with an instrument called a vigorimeter.

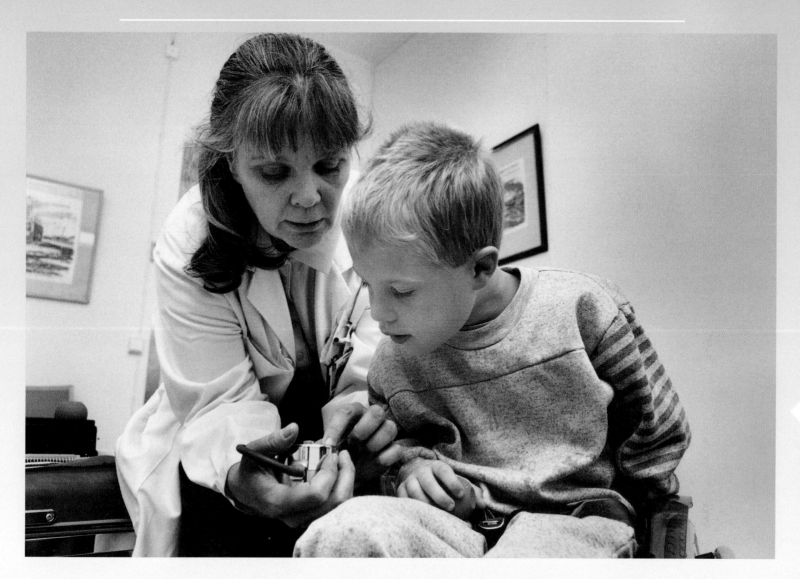

Dr. Mia tells Stefan and his mother about new research and treatments that are available for muscular dystrophy. Stefan is given a new medicine that hopefully will increase his strength and endurance.

Stefan has known Dr. Mia six years now, and they like each other very much.

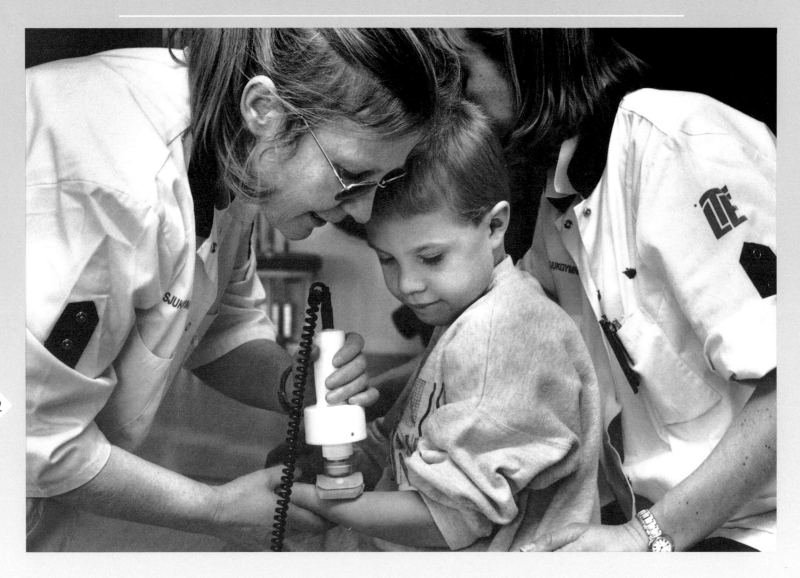

Next, Stefan has an appointment with two physical therapists, Mette and Kicki. They measure the strength of Stefan's muscles at different times to see if the medicine is working and helping him. They test the strength of his feet, legs, arms, and shoulders with an instrument called a myometer.

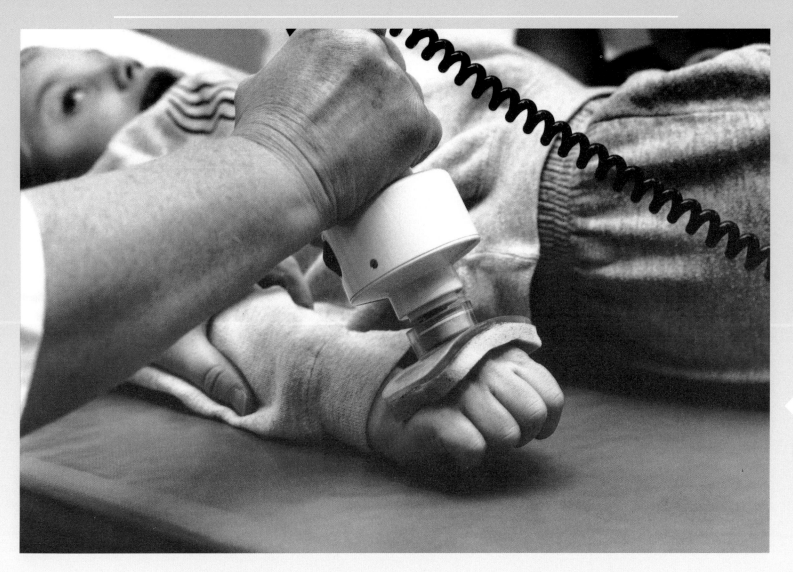

Like any boy, Stefan wants to be strong, and he is very eager to get good results. He grabs the myometer with both hands even though he knows only one arm will be tested at a time. Stefan expects good results, but he is disappointed.

Today, Stefan is going to receive his very own wheelcar. He has been looking forward to this special day for a long time! Stefan loves to go fast. His mother watches him drive the wheelcar with concern for his safety, but there is no need to worry. Stefan is a careful driver, and he does well. "This is my very best birthday present!" he says, although it is not his birthday.

Stefan's family has a collie named Rocky. Rocky always watches Stefan while he plays. If someone talks too loud to Stefan or is too rough with him, Rocky barks out a warning. Rocky sleeps at the foot of Stefan's bed. The loyal dog often stays there overnight until Stefan wakes up in the morning. When they first see each other, Stefan and Rocky hug and kiss. Rocky is adored by the entire family.

In the summer, Stefan plays in a wading pool in his yard. His friend Jesper joins him sometimes. Stefan's mother carries him to the pool. The boys splash each other. Now and then, Stefan falls under the water. But with a little help from Jesper and by holding onto the edge of the pool, Stefan manages to come up again. Stefan gets on his feet by supporting himself with his hands on his legs. He then pulls away as hard as he can and stands straight.

Standing up will get harder as Stefan's muscles get weaker.

"Mother," Stefan cries. "I can't get up from the porch. Come and help me, quickly, please!" Stefan's arms and legs have become much weaker lately. He is tired of having to ask for help all the time. He wants to manage on his own. When he fails, he often gets angry and sad.

"I'm so afraid of falling," Stefan says. "It feels as if my legs give way under me like a pocketknife."

Besides his toy trucks, Stefan also enjoys playing with his toy motorcycles and dinosaurs. He gets very excited when talking about Apatosaurus (or Brontosaurus), one of the biggest dinosaurs that ever lived. It ate only plants and grew as long as 66 feet (20 meters). "That's longer than my dad's big truck with a trailer," Stefan says. Stefan's favorite dinosaur is Stegosaurus. It had very long hind legs and a big, spiked tail for defense.

Stefan collects model dinosaurs and reads fascinating books about dinosaurs. The subject of dinosaurs keeps Stefan entertained for hours.

"Sandra is my little sister and my very best friend," Stefan says. "We play and have a lot of fun together. Sandra helps me tie my shoestrings. When I fall down, she fetches Mother, and they lift me up."

Sandra always stands up for Stefan if someone says something nasty about him or to him. But sometimes Sandra wants to be alone with her girlfriend. This makes Stefan jealous, angry, and sad. He feels left out because he sits in his wheelcar and is unable to walk and run around like the other children. But Sandra has never criticized Stefan about his condition. She gives him a hug and says, "You are the very best big brother of all."

Stefan pulls himself up into his wheelcar and drives to the playground.
He gets out of the car on his own and climbs down the vehicle. He crawls to
the monkey bars and tries to climb up, but he cannot do it. There is nobody
there to help him. So Stefan crawls back to his car and, with one hand at a
time, slowly climbs up into the seat. He fastens his seat belt and drives back
home again. He is so exhausted that he cannot get out of the car by himself.
His mother helps him. He rests for several hours afterward.

Stefan goes to a school called Ekebyhov, and he is in a small class.
He likes his classmates. Ann-Sofie does some arithmetic with Stefan.
"I like to work with someone," says Stefan. The two students have a
good time learning together.

Stefan also likes his teacher Ann-Christine and his assistant Charles very
much. "They are all so nice to me," says Stefan. Stefan likes writing and
doing arithmetic, but his hand often gets tired. Then he uses the computer.

Stefan also has a computer at home. He uses it to do his homework and
to play.

26

This afternoon, Charles pays a visit to Stefan. Charles arrives on his motorbike. Charles is Stefan's assistant at school. He helps Stefan with anything he is unable to do by himself. They enjoy being together and are good friends. Charles even takes Stefan with him to motorbike races.

Stefan is allowed to sit on Charles's motorbike only when it is standing still. Unfortunately, Stefan's arm muscles are too weak to sit behind Charles and hold on to him while the motorbike is in motion.

"It's still cool," says Stefan.

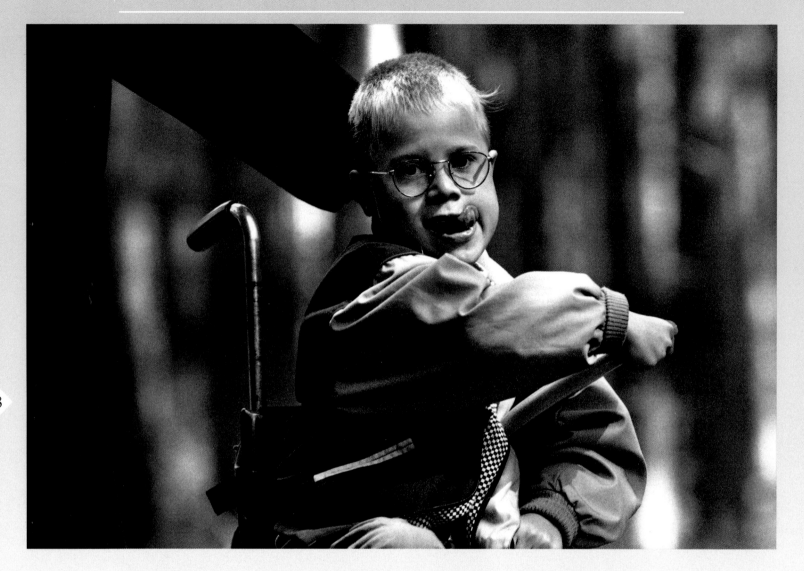

Stefan's class is going on a field trip today. The physical education teacher has prepared a trail in the forest with various activities along the way. In addition, the students will learn the importance of taking good care of the environment.

There are fifteen different checkpoints altogether. At one checkpoint, the children are supposed to throw a Frisbee. Stefan enjoys this activity, even though he is not able to throw the Frisbee as far as the other children.

Charles cannot throw the Frisbee at all. He has become tired after pushing Stefan up and down several small hills in a wheelchair. After a break and something to eat, everyone is ready for new adventures.

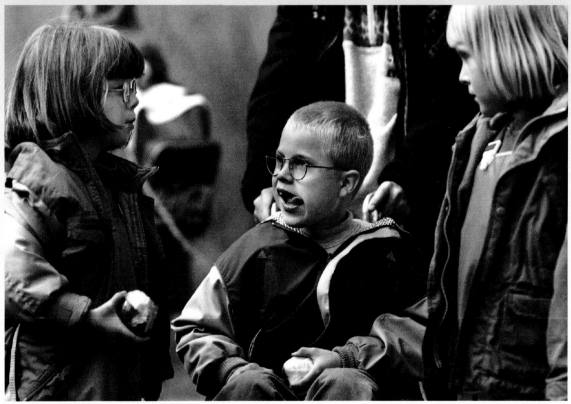

Twice a week, Stefan takes lessons in handicrafts at school. His teacher's name is Monica. Today, Stefan has decided to create a bath towel for himself. He has chosen a gray one.

Stefan draws a picture of Donald Duck in the middle of the towel. He then cuts out some pieces of fabric in different colors for Donald Duck's face, nose, and cap. He sews the pieces onto the towel.

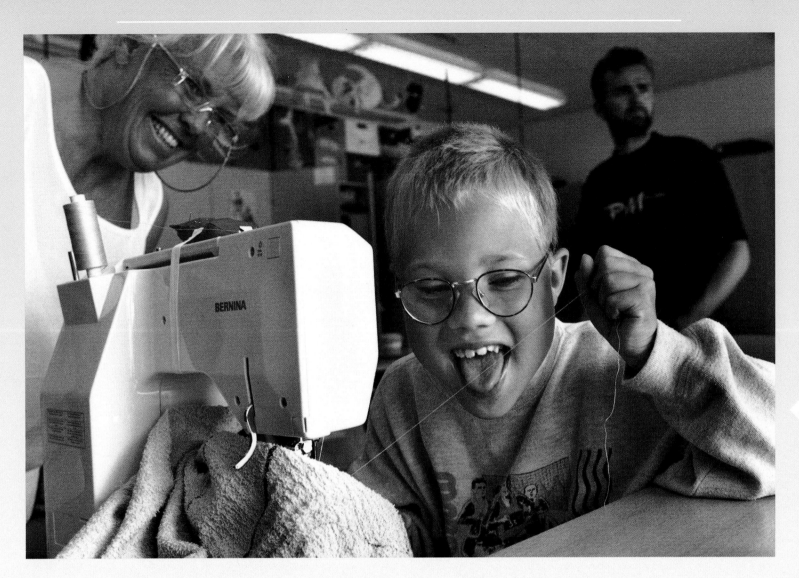

"Come and have a look," Stefan says to his teacher. "I sewed Donald's face onto the towel with the sewing machine all by myself. I like working with the motorbike, no, I mean the sewing machine! It is just like a motorbike. You can drive fast or slow down."

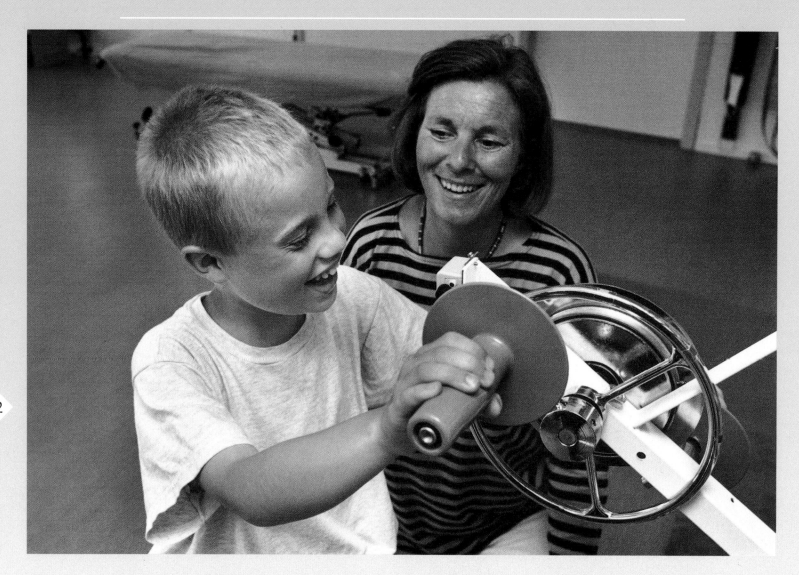

Stefan likes visiting his physical therapist Anette. His visits with her last about one hour. "She is always cheerful and works very hard with me," says Stefan.

Anette has prepared a small course for Stefan to maneuver. Making his way through the course will exercise several different muscles. Exercise can slow down Stefan's disease and make him feel good.

After finishing the course, Stefan lies down. Anette stretches his thigh muscles and Achilles tendons. Stefan finishes the session by playing in the swimming pool.

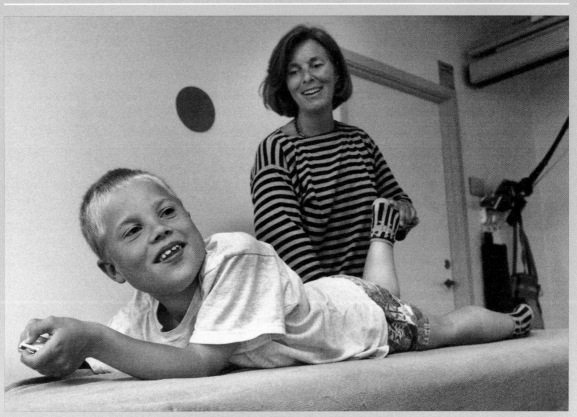

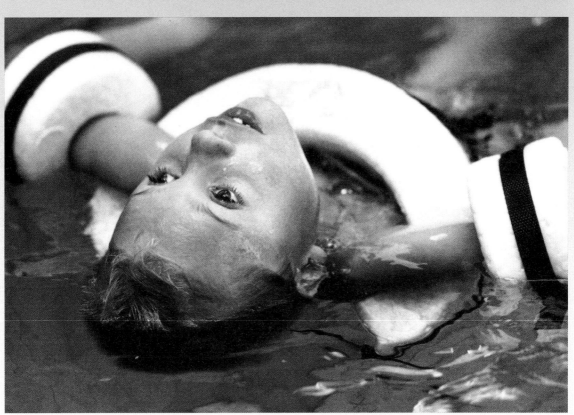

Stefan has just come home from a long day in school and a visit to his physical therapist. He feels warm and sweaty and wants to take a bath.

The bathroom has a lifting device that makes it much easier for Stefan to get in and out of the bathtub. Stefan's mother helps him get into the sling.

As his mother lowers him into the tub, Stefan says sadly to his mother, "Last year, I could get in and out of the tub by myself. But now I no longer can."

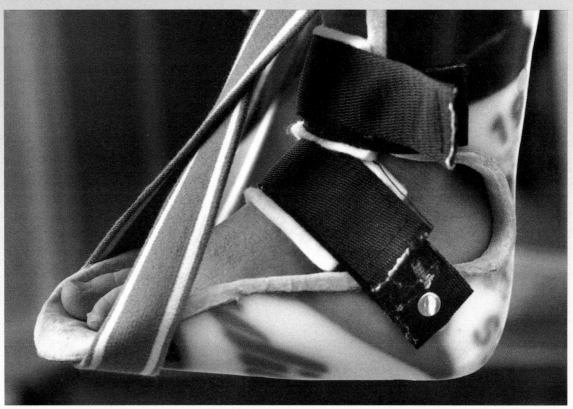

Before Stefan goes to sleep, Sandra comes running into his room. She jumps onto his bed. Their mother reads a story to them every evening at bedtime. Tonight, she reads *The Lion King*.

Stefan has his night splints on, as usual. He has to wear them every night to keep his Achilles tendons from getting shorter. If they became shorter, Stefan would find it even harder to walk. He hates the splints. They make his feet so warm. But Stefan must put up with them anyway.

Before drifting off to sleep, Stefan carefully looks around his room. He wants all his things to be in the right place to make it easier for him to get up in the morning.

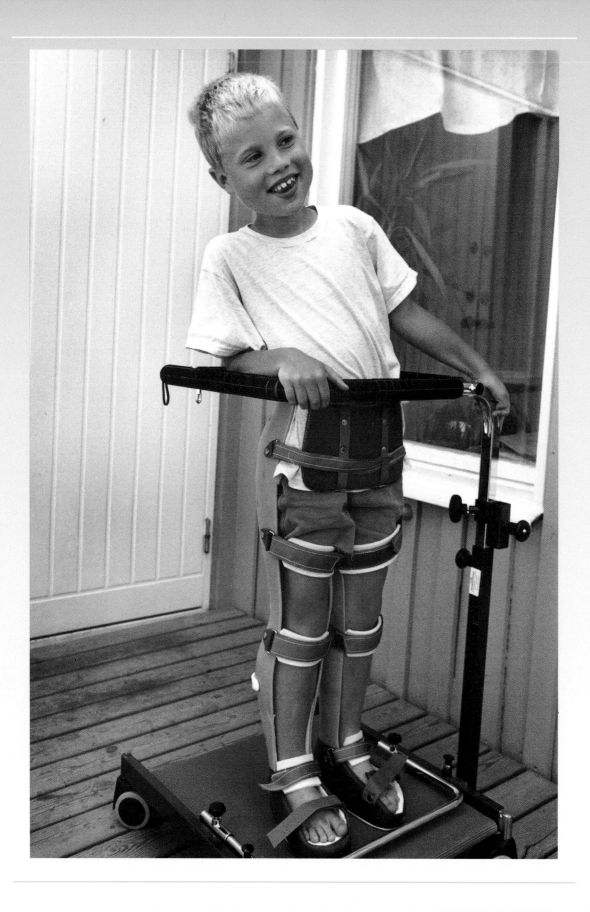

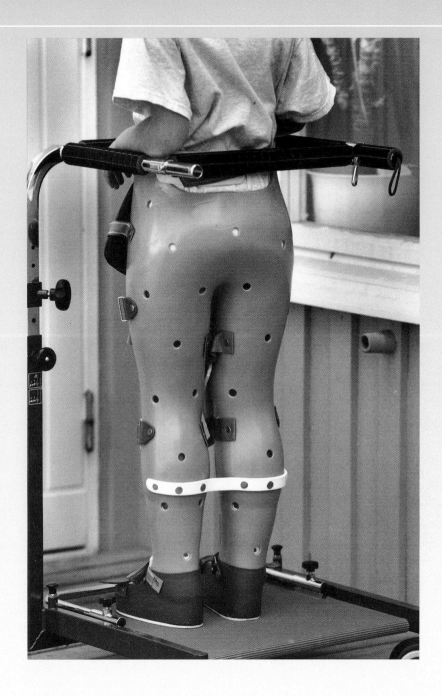

In Stefan's home, there are various objects that help him live as normal a life as possible. One such object is called a standing shell. It is a cast of his body. Stefan is not very fond of it because it makes him feel too restricted. Stefan's mother often has to nag him to use it.

But Stefan knows why he must use the standing shell a little while every day. Working with the shell allows him to exercise his back muscles. It prevents him from developing a curvature of the spine called scoliosis.

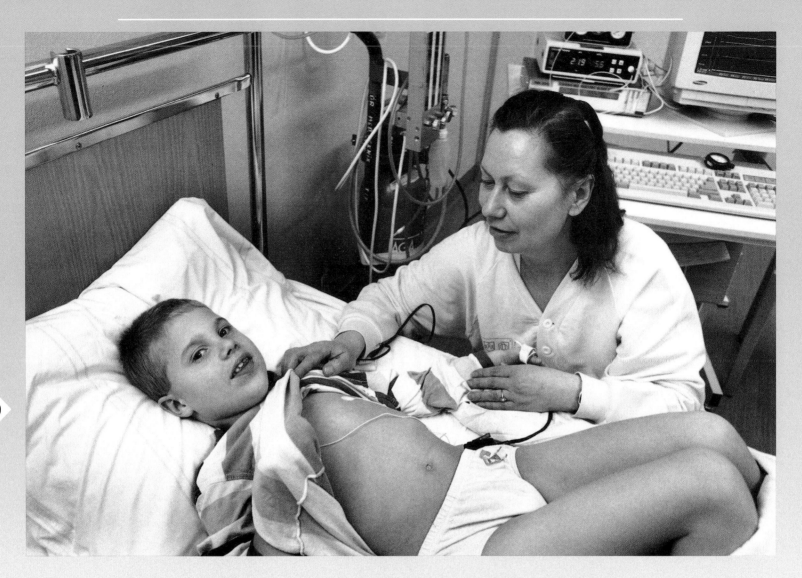

Tonight, Stefan and his mother go to the hospital so Stefan can take a breathing test. A nurse named Siv welcomes Stefan and tells him what is going to happen.

Siv connects some rubber cords to Stefan's chest and one to his left thumb. Then she must wait for Stefan to fall asleep. Stefan's mother reads a book to him, and he soon falls asleep.

A computer measures and registers Stefan's breathing. It indicates how deep he is sleeping; whether or not he is snoring; and whether or not he is exhaling, or breathing out, properly.

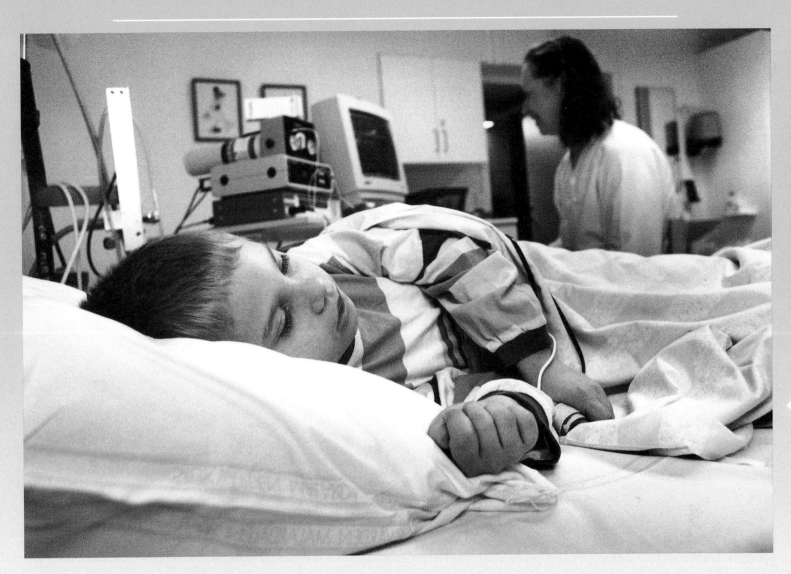

When Stefan wakes up the next morning, the test is finished. All the results are good, except one. While sleeping very deeply, he did not breathe out hard enough to free himself of carbon dioxide. This could make him feel tired.

Still, Dr. Mia is satisfied with the results.

One evening, Stefan and his mother talk about life. Stefan has many questions about his own life and his future.

Stefan asks, "Why could I walk up the stairs at granddad's house last summer, but not today? I could swing on the playground all by myself before, but I cannot do that anymore. I cannot even get up from the toilet by myself."

It is very hard for Stefan's mother to answer all his questions. She knows that a child should be able to grow and then crawl, walk, run, and play as hard as he or she wants.

Stefan's family hopes that soon a new medicine will be found to stop the progression of the disease. If only the hands of time could be stopped!

The family wishes that everybody could see Stefan beyond his muscular dystrophy — as the fine and bright boy he really is, with a gleam in his eyes and a big, warm heart.

QUESTIONS ABOUT MUSCULAR DYSTROPHY

Sometimes we can become confused or upset by people who are different from us. Getting the answers to any questions we may have about other people is one way of gaining understanding about them. Here are some of the most frequently asked questions about muscular dystrophy.

What is muscular dystrophy?
Muscular dystrophy is a term given to a group of diseases that causes a gradual wasting away of muscle that leads to weakness and disability.

How common is muscular dystrophy?
There are about 250,000 people with muscular dystrophy in the United States alone. About two-thirds of them are children. The most common childhood form, Duchenne muscular dystrophy, occurs in about one in every 3,500 newborn boys.

What muscles does muscular dystrophy affect?
It can affect any of the muscles, but the spinal musculature and the limb girdles (the shoulders and hips) are most commonly affected.

In what area of the world can the most cases of muscular dystrophy be found?
Muscular dystrophy is found in every nation. No one area has more cases than any other.

Can a person catch muscular dystrophy?
No. Muscular dystrophy is congenital. This means a person is born with the gene flaw that causes it. It may be transferred from one or both parents to their child through their genes, or it may occur because a flaw develops in a baby's genes before birth.

Is there any way for adults who have the gene to know they have it?
Blood tests and medical examinations can indicate who carries the gene in some forms of the disease.

What are the types of muscular dystrophy called?
The main types are: Duchenne, Becker, facioscapulohumeral, limb-girdle, and myotonic.

Can both boys and girls get muscular dystrophy?
Most forms of muscular dystrophy can affect either boys or girls. However, Duchenne and Becker dystrophies usually affect boys.

Can a child with muscular dystrophy attend regular school?
Yes, most children can, but they may require assistance. Some children with muscular dystrophy even go on to college.

What is the most common type of muscular dystrophy?
The most common type in children is called Duchenne. It was first described in 1861 by a French physician named Guillaume-Benjamin-Amand Duchenne. Symptoms of Duchenne muscular dystrophy usually appear in children between the ages of two and six. The most common type of adult muscular dystrophy is myotonic dystrophy.

Is it possible to tell if a newborn has muscular dystrophy?
The weakness and wasting of muscles associated with muscular dystrophy is usually not apparent until the child is older. But it is possible to test a newborn's muscle enzyme level. The results may indicate the presence of Duchenne or Becker muscular dystrophy.

Can older children get muscular dystrophy?
Yes, and so can adults. Symptoms of limb-girdle, Emery-Dreifuss, and facioscapulohumeral muscular dystrophy often don't appear until late childhood or the teens. Other forms, including myotonic dystrophy, may not be obvious until adulthood.

What are the first warning signs of Duchenne muscular dystrophy?
Neck muscles and the large muscles of the legs and the lower trunk are the first to become weak. Over time, the upper trunk and arms and eventually all the major muscle groups weaken.

The first signs are frequent falling, difficulty doing a standing jump, toe walking, a protruding abdomen, difficulty rising from the floor, lordosis (the inward curve of the back), the inability to run, and a waddling walk. Later signs include difficulty in rising from a chair, the inability to climb stairs normally, and a wide walk accompanied by difficulty with balance.

What are the first warning signs of muscular dystrophy in an adult?
In facioscapulohumeral dystrophy, the adult has a weak smile and the inability to pucker the lips or to whistle. In limb-girdle dystrophy, there is weakness in the shoulders and hips. Early signs of myotonic dystrophy include weakness of the feet and hands and difficulty in relaxing a grip of the hands.

When a person has muscular dystrophy, are they in pain?
No. Muscular dystrophy is associated with weakness and disability, not pain.

Is there a cure for muscular dystrophy?
Unfortunately, there is no cure as yet for any form of the disease, but a lot can be done to reduce its effects. Prevention of deformity, active orthopedic treatment, physical therapy, and sometimes respiratory support serve to increase function, improve quality of life, and extend life expectancy.

What are some of the treatments for muscular dystrophy?
Leg braces enable the individual to stand and walk and not tire so easily. Leg stretches keep the muscles limber. Surgery can lengthen contracted tendons to temporarily strengthen muscles.

How do physical therapists help a person with muscular dystrophy?
Physical therapists keep the individual's muscles stretched out. They also teach various exercises to improve the individual's well being.

How do occupational therapists help a person with muscular dystrophy?
Occupational therapists help the individual with everyday tasks. They teach new ways to eat, play, get dressed, and participate in other activities.

Can certain prescription drugs treat muscular dystrophy?
Drugs can relieve muscle stiffness or slow progress of the disease in some cases. However, no drug therapy exists as yet for muscle weakness. Researchers are trying to develop drugs that can be used to increase strength and endurance.

If there is not yet a cure for muscular dystrophy, why is it important to diagnose the disease early?
It is important so that the individual and the family can receive assistance at a care center that has the latest treatments and information about any advances toward a cure. It is also important so that the individual can establish contact with a care center for physical, psychological, and social support. In addition, it is important so that the individual's parents and other relatives can receive counseling regarding any future pregnancies.

Does muscular dystrophy get worse and worse in an individual?
Yes. The disease progresses over time. However, there are times when normal growth and development in a child seem to give the child added strength.

In Duchenne muscular dystrophy, muscle weakness begins to advance rapidly after the age of eight or nine. Then, leg braces may be necessary so the child can stand or walk. A wheelchair or wheelcar is usually needed by or before early adolescence.

What begins to happen at advanced stages of muscular dystrophy?
Muscles shorten around the joints, the spine curves, and lung capacity weakens. Those with Duchenne rarely live beyond their twenties.

What is being done to find a cure?
Scientists funded by the Muscular Dystrophy Association have discovered the causes of several forms of muscular dystrophy. Duchenne dystrophy is caused when a gene fails to manufacture an important protein called dystrophin. Becker dystrophy results when the same gene doesn't make enough dystrophin or makes an abnormal form of it. This protein is necessary for proper muscle growth and functioning. MDA scientists also know which gene defects cause myotonic, facioscapulohumeral,

and limb-girdle dystrophies. Now that scientists know what causes muscular dystrophy, they are working hard to find ways to correct what goes wrong and cure the disease. One means is by gene therapy — inserting a properly functioning gene manufactured in a laboratory into a person's muscles. Researchers are experimenting to find a safe and practical way to do gene therapy in people.

What is the Muscular Dystrophy Association?
MDA is a voluntary health agency that is a partnership between scientists and concerned citizens dedicated to medical research in the area of muscular dystrophy. Its goal is to find cures or treatments for the forty neuromuscular diseases in its program. It was formed in 1950 by a small group of parents whose children had muscular dystrophy. The Muscular Dystrophy Association operates outpatient clinics to meet the medical and personal needs of people living with muscular dystrophy. MDA helps provide orthopedic aids, educational guidance, counseling, recreational programs, transportation, and various other forms of support.

THINGS TO DO AND THINK ABOUT

By doing these projects, you'll learn more about people living with muscular dystrophy and other medical situations.

1. Do you know someone who has muscular dystrophy? If so, make a point of talking with that person about the effects the condition has had on her or his life. What sort of special routine does your friend have to follow? Does your friend have to go to the doctor a lot?

2. Read more books about muscular dystrophy. Keep up on the latest scientific findings and treatments.

3. From reading this book, do you think you'd be

interested in becoming a doctor, nurse, physical therapist, or occupational therapist?

4. Volunteer to help someone in need, whatever the special circumstances, whenever possible.

5. When the telethon for the Muscular Dystrophy Association is on television over Labor Day weekend, get together with your friends to watch it. Do some chores and errands in the neighborhood to earn money and make a pledge to help find a cure for muscular dystrophy.

WHERE TO WRITE OR CALL FOR MORE INFORMATION

The following organizations can give you further information about muscular dystrophy. If you write, be sure to include a stamped, self-addressed envelope for a reply.

In the United States, write or call the Muscular Dystrophy Association office nearest you; or write or call the national office at:
Muscular Dystrophy Association
3300 East Sunrise Drive
Tucson, AZ 85718-3208
1-800-572-1717

Muscular Dystrophy Association of Canada –
National Office
2345 Yonge Street
Suite 900
Toronto, Ontario M4P 2E5
(416) 488-0030

Muscular Dystrophy Association
of New South Wales
G.P.O. 9932
Sydney, N.S.W. Australia 2001
(02) 360-3438

Muscular Dystrophy Association
of New Zealand
P. O. Box 23-047
Papatoetoe, Auckland   New Zealand
(09) 278-7216

On Your Computer:
CompuServe: MDA Forum – Type "Go MDA."

MORE READING MATERIAL ABOUT MUSCULAR DYSTROPHY

The publications listed below provide in-depth material about muscular dystrophy.

Mainstream: Magazine of the Able-Disabled
Go! Guide (Disability Products and Resources)
Mainstream, P. O. Box 370598
San Diego, CA 92137-0598

Muscular Dystrophy. James A. Corrick
   (Venture Books, Franklin Watts)

Quest is the national magazine of the
   Muscular Dystrophy Association
   3300 East Sunrise Drive
   Tucson, AZ 85718-3208

Muscular Dystrophy: The Facts.
   Alan E. H. Emery, M.D. (Oxford University Press)

Muscular Dystrophy Association (U.S.) pamphlets include:

Everybody's Different, Nobody's Perfect

Hey! I'm Here, Too!
   (for siblings of children with muscular dystrophy)

You Are Not Alone
   (for parents of a child with muscular dystrophy)

Facts about Muscular Dystrophy

Learning to Live with Neuromuscular Disease:
   A Message for Parents

A Teacher's Guide to Duchenne Muscular Dystrophy

GLOSSARY OF WORDS ABOUT MUSCULAR DYSTROPHY

Achilles tendon: the strong tendon that joins the muscles in the calf of the leg to the bone of the heel.

carbon dioxide: the gas that humans and animals breathe out and plants absorb.

congenital: a condition that exists at birth.

disabling: a condition that restricts a person's abilities and capacities.

Duchenne: the most common childhood type of muscular dystrophy. It was first described by a French physician named Guillaume-Benjamin-Amand Duchenne in 1861.

muscular dystrophy: a group of diseases that causes a gradual wasting away of muscle that leads to weakness and disability.

myometer: a medical instrument that tests for muscle strength in the feet, legs, arms, and shoulders.

night splints: rigid supports worn on the legs to keep Achilles tendons stretched.

physical therapist: a person in the medical field who treats disease through physical means, such as stretching and exercises.

scoliosis: curvature of the spine.

standing shell: a rigid apparatus that allows people with muscular dystrophy to exercise their back muscles, thereby preventing scoliosis.

vigorimeter: a medical instrument that tests muscle strength in the hands.

48

INDEX